# Word

## God Speaks to Us

The Lutheran Spirituality Series

**John T. Pless**

CONCORDIA PUBLISHING HOUSE · SAINT LOUIS

# Contents

About This Series ........................................ 4

Participant Introduction ............................... 5

    The God Who Speaks ............................. 7

    The Words That Kill and Give Life ............. 12

    Word and Spirit ..................................... 18

    Inwardly Digesting the Word ..................... 23

    Praying the Word .................................. 28

    The Comfort of the Word ......................... 32

Leader Guide Introduction ............................ 36

    Answers ............................................. 37

Appendix of Lutheran Teaching ..................... 58

Glossary ............................................... 61

| Hymnal Key |
| --- |
| *LSB=Lutheran Service Book* |
| *ELH=Evangelical Lutheran Hymnary* |
| *CW=Christian Worship* |
| *LW=Lutheran Worship* |
| *LBW=Lutheran Book of Worship* |
| *TLH=The Lutheran Hymnal* |

# About This Series

In the West, spirituality is as nebulous as it is popular. Having succumbed to humanism, rationalism, and Darwinism, communities once known for a genuine Christian piety now provide a fertile breeding ground for self-made theologies, Eastern religions, the worship of science and technology, or even a resuscitation of the old pagan gods. In a highly competitive environment, each of these spiritual philosophies seeks to fill the vacuum left by the seemingly departed Christian spirit.

Even among faithful Christians, and at other times and places, spirituality has run the gamut from the mystical to the almost sterile. From the emotional to the pragmatic, the experiential to the cerebral, the all-too-human desire to experience (and control!) the divine has proven to be especially resilient. Influenced by modernism, postmodernism, and whatever comes next, even those who try faithfully to follow Jesus Christ may find defining *spirituality*, or at least what is distinctively Christian about their own beliefs and practices, a significant challenge.

Do Lutheran Christians have a spirituality? Indeed they do! This adult Bible study series explores the rich depths of a distinctively Lutheran spirituality that begins in Baptism and is founded upon God's Word. There, the incarnate, crucified, and resurrected Lord proclaims His victory over sin, death, and the devil, and from there flows the proclamation of His Gospel and the administration of His Sacraments. It is through these means presented within the liturgy of His Church that Christ communicates not merely spiritual energies, an emotional high, a method of reasoning, or a stringent morality, but truly Himself—God in human flesh.

Written by respected Lutheran scholars in the United States and Australia, this adult Bible study series emphasizes the Bible, Luther's catechism, and the Lutheran hymnal as concrete and integral resources for a truly Lutheran spirituality. May God richly bless those who study His Word, and through His Word may they experience the genuinely enlightening and life-giving spirituality found only in the life, death, and resurrection of our Lord and Savior, Jesus Christ.

The Editor

4

# Participant Introduction

Our God is a speaking God. Unlike idols made of mute stone or crafted by the imaginations of the faithless heart, the living God has a voice. He speaks and His words are "spirit and life" (John 6:63). By His strong Word, the Father brought creation into existence. His Word made flesh is the revelation of His fatherly goodness and the author of our salvation, for He was sent to suffer and die as our Savior. The Word of our Savior's cross, the message of reconciliation in the forgiveness of sins, is preached for the creation of faith as "faith comes from hearing, and hearing through the word of Christ" (Romans 10:17). The same Spirit given by Jesus to His apostles on Easter evening (see John 20:22) inspired them to put the Word into writing "so that you might believe that Jesus is the Christ, the Son of God, and that by believing you may have life in His name" (John 20:31).

Lutheran spirituality is a spirituality of the Word. God's Spirit ties Himself to His Word. We do not look behind or above the Scriptures to find the Spirit, but rather we listen to the Spirit who speaks to us in Christ Jesus. There is no other Jesus than the one proclaimed by the prophets and the apostles. A nineteenth-century hymn of non-Lutheran origin says "Beyond the sacred page I seek you, Lord." However, believers do not look beyond the sacred page of the Scriptures to find the Lord. The Lord Jesus is wrapped up in the words of Holy Scripture. To hear its words is to hear Him, for He is the very heart and core of the Bible.

This study is designed as a hearing aid. That is, it is the purpose of this little book to assist you not only in understanding what God's Word is and how it functions, but also to sharpen your skills in listening to our Lord as He speaks in His Scriptures and in preaching that is governed by the Scriptures. To understand the Scriptures is to *stand under* the Scriptures. It is not so much that we interpret the Scriptures but that the Scriptures interpret our lives. With God's Law, they convict us of sin, that is, of unbelief. They interpret the story of our inborn failure to fear, love, and trust in God above all things as the root of all sin. But the ultimate message of the Bible is the Gospel, God's own declaration that He is *for us* in every way, bestowing on us the forgiveness of sins achieved by His Son's death on the cross. Any reading of the Bible that does not end up with Jesus Christ crucified and raised for our justification misses the mark, for God's Scriptures were given "to make you wise for salvation through faith in Christ Jesus" (2 Timothy 3:15). Keep your copy of Luther's Small Catechism and your hymnal close at hand as you embark on this study, for they are the two most important tools that you have to help you stand sure-footed under the Holy Scriptures.

Lurking in these pages you will see the footprints of Martin Luther. He charted a course for us to follow in learning how to listen to the Scriptures. From Psalm 119, Luther drew three rules for the study of the Bible: *oratio, meditatio, tentatio.* Scriptures are prayerfully read (*oratio*) as that book "which turns the wisdom of all other books into foolishness" (AE 34:285), meditated upon in faith (*meditatio*), and held on to for life in the face of all that threatens us with death (*tentatio*). That's how students of the Scriptures are made. Let Luther's three rules guide your reading of God's Word as well, for such a reading promises to yield rich fruit as God's truth is implanted in ear and heart and lives are tested and made strong under the cross.

Some of you may wish to dig deeper into the Lutheran confession of God's gift of Holy Scriptures. For those of you who wish to do so, two resources are recommended: Robert Preus's *The Inspiration of Scripture* (CPH) and Armin Wenz's, "Justification and Holy Scripture: *Sola fide et sola Scriptura*" in *Logia: A Journal of Lutheran Theology* XIV, no. 2 (Eastertide 2005), pages 5–15.

To prepare for "The God Who Speaks," read Hebrews 1:1–2.

# The God Who Speaks

*Dearest Jesus, at your word we have come again to hear you; Let our thoughts and hearts be stirred and in glowing faith be near you as the promises here given draw us wholly up to heaven.*

Tobias Clausnitzer, *Lutheran Worship,* 202

The Holy Scriptures therefore are nothing less than the on-going pentecost-miracle, as Martin Kähler once wrote. In a world where many voices become audible, where truth and error form an inseparable mish-mash, God's highest gift to mankind is the sure foundation which the Spirit has laid for us in the unchanging writings of the prophets and the apostles. It is God himself who verifies and falsifies our theology, who destroys our errors and establishes our faith and theology, through the infallible word of the Scriptures. (Armin Wenz, "Justification and Holy Scripture," *Logia* XIV, no. 2 [Eastertide 2005]: p. 9)

In this session we will look at the Scriptures that tell us of God and what He has to say to human beings. As we have noted in the Introduction, God is a speaking God; He is not silent. But the deafening clamor of our sinful nature and the subtle accents of the devil's beguiling speech may drown out the voice of the Good Shepherd.

1. What things are most likely to get in the way of your hearing God's Word?

## By the Prophets

In the Nicene Creed, we confess that the Holy Spirit "spoke by the prophets." Here the creed echoes such texts as Hebrews 1:1–2 and

Luke 24:25–48. These passages testify that the Old Testament writings are the Word of God and that they point to and are fulfilled in Jesus, who came in our flesh to suffer and die for the sins of the world. After our Lord's resurrection from the dead, He opens the minds of His disciples to understand the Scriptures.

2. What are some of the ways that God spoke to His people in the Old Testament? See Genesis 12:1–3; 15:1; Exodus 3:1–12; 1 Kings 19:9–18; and Jeremiah 1:1–10.

3. Read 1 Samuel 3:1–18. How does Samuel receive the Word of the Lord?

4. As we have observed in several Old Testament texts, God often used visions as the instrument of His voice to the prophets. According to Hebrews 1:1–2, where does God speak to us now? How would this passage help in addressing people in our own day who claim to have heard God in a dream?

5. What does the Old Testament indicate about the Messiah according to Luke 24:45–47?

6. How does Hebrews 1:2 describe God's Son?

7. Read Genesis 1:3–5 and John 1:1–3. What did God do through His Word? Who is this Word?

## Listening to the Son

The Transfiguration of Jesus (read Luke 9:28–36) demonstrates Jesus' identity and shows Him to be the fulfillment of the Law and the Prophets. This event in the life of our Lord comes to a climax as the Father speaks out of the cloud: "This is My Son, My Chosen One; listen to Him!" (v. 35).

8. Moses and Elijah appear on the mountain with Jesus. What is the significance of these two figures from the Old Testament? What do they speak to Jesus about?

9. What does the Transfiguration tell us about the origin and use of the Scriptures? See 2 Peter 1:16–21. There are Christian denominations that diminish the place of Scripture by arguing that it is historically-conditioned or bound to an ancient culture and so not applicable to us today. How would you answer this charge? How does such diminishing of Scripture make Christ less of a Savior than He is?

## Where Do We Hear God?

The Holy Scriptures and Christian preaching go hand in hand. Luther called the Church a "mouth house" rather than a "pen house" as a way of stressing the oral character of God's Word. God caused His Word to be put into writing, and thereby He gave it a fixed and permanent location in order that it might be proclaimed truthfully through all generations. The Bible is not just a book about God, and preaching is not just talk about God. In and through both the Scriptures and the sermon, God is speaking. The aim of His speaking is to bestow the forgiveness of sins, to bring life out of death.

10. In the Divine Service, there is a sequence that follows from the reading of the Old Testament, Epistle, and Holy Gospel culminating in the sermon. How does this ordering demonstrate the connection between God's written Word and His proclaimed Word?

11. Read Luke 10:16. Preaching is the living voice of the Gospel as it conforms to Holy Scripture in proclaiming the forgiveness of sins for Christ's sake. When we hear such preaching, who are we hearing?

## Spiritual Exercises

- Spend some time next Saturday evening reading the appointed lectionary for the Divine Service on Sunday. How is God's Law operative in these texts to unmask your own sin? How is God's Gospel at work to forgive your sins and comfort you with Christ's promises?
- Review Luther's explanation to the Third Commandment in the Small Catechism. Luther does not focus on the Sabbath day per se, for the requirement of a specific day for worship has been fulfilled in Christ. Instead, Luther contends that we are not to "despise preaching and His Word, but hold it sacred and gladly hear and learn it." Let the Third Commandment and its explanation be part of your Saturday evening preparation for the Divine Service.
- Pray Psalm 119:33–40 each day in the coming week as you ask God to instruct you with His words and confirm in you the promises of His Gospel.

# Point to Remember

Truly, truly, I say to you, whoever hears my word and believes him who sent me has eternal life. He does not come into judgment, but has passed from death to life. John 5:24

To prepare for "The Words That Kill and Give Life," read 2 Corinthians 3:7–11.

# The Words That Kill and Give Life

*I learned to distinguish between the righteousness of the law and the righteousness of the gospel, I lacked nothing before this except that I made no distinction between the law and gospel. I regarded both as the same thing and held that there was no difference between Christ and Moses except the times in which they lived and their degrees of perfection. But when I discovered the proper distinction—namely, that the law is one thing and the gospel another—I made myself free.*

Martin Luther, AE 54:442–43

God speaks in two completely different voices to us in the Scripture. His Law is the preaching of wrath against sin. It is that voice from Sinai's lofty heights that thunders with condemnation of the sinner and his sin. The Gospel stands in distinct contrast from the Law. While the Law makes demands and threatens with punishment, the Gospel makes promises and bespeaks peace with God in the blood of Jesus Christ. The Bible is misused when the Law is not clearly distinguished from the Gospel. The Bible is misused when Law and Gospel are not used together to teach and meditate. If Jesus is transformed into something other than a Savior, and seen only as a "new Moses," a spiritual coach, a teacher of moral precepts, or the pattern for the pious life, the Bible is misused and the Gospel is abandoned. Lutheran spirituality practices the highest art of all: rightly reading the Scriptures so that threat is distinguished from God's promises in Christ Jesus.

12. C. F. W. Walther writes, "Rightly distinguishing the Law and the Gospel is the most difficult and the highest art of Christians in general and of theologians in particular. It is taught only by the Holy Spirit in the school of experience" (*Law and Gospel*, trans. W. H.

T. Dau [CPH 1929, 1986], p. 42). In your own experience as a believer, what makes this distinction so difficult?

# A Life and Death Distinction

In the passage that you read in preparation for this session, 2 Corinthians 3:7–11, the apostle Paul describes the office of the Law as "the ministry of death." In contrast, Paul describes the office of the Gospel as "the ministry of the Spirit" (v. 8). The ministry of death results in condemnation, for the Law convicts and executes sinners who live in opposition to God, trusting in themselves. The ministry of the Spirit is called "the ministry of righteousness" (v. 9) because it serves the redeeming work of Christ Jesus, who justifies the ungodly, declaring them righteous through faith in His atoning sacrifice. The ministry of death has a fading glory. It finds its end in Jesus who was put to death for our sin and raised to life for our justification. His Gospel, therefore, has a permanent glory because Christ's victory over sin, death, and the devil is eternal. Death will never put Jesus back in the grave. He lives to impart life in the forgiveness of sins to all who trust the promise of His Gospel.

Now we turn to Romans 3:19–31, where Paul demonstrates what is at stake in the right distinction of the Law and the Gospel.

13. According to verse 19, to whom does the Law speak?

14. Look at verse 20. What will the Law not do? What will it do?

13

15. What is the "righteousness of God" (v. 21) and how is it made manifest?

16. What is the basis for our justification? What role does faith have?

17. Justification is received, not achieved. What does this do to human boasting?

18. What does justification "by faith apart from the works of the law" (v. 28) do to the Law?

## To Mix Is to Muddle

To mix the Law and the Gospel is to loose both. When the Gospel is blended with the Law, we are deceived into thinking that with the right amount of willpower, discipline, perseverance, and effort we can make ourselves right before God. Likewise, when the Law is seen as an additive to the Gospel, Christ Jesus becomes less of a Savior and more of an example. There is no good news in an offer of salvation that depends on emulating Christ. In fact, we would be lost from the start. Who of us has been born of a virgin and lived a life of complete perfection without sin? Sinners do not need a teacher or an example, sinners need a Savior. That is exactly what God has given us in His Son.

In reading the Scriptures and in speaking God's Word, we are to distinguish the Law from the Gospel. The Law comes by way of demand. It speaks to what we must do or leave undone. The Gospel is never about what I must do, but about what God has done and what He continues to do for me, as my Savior. As you read the Bible, pay attention to who it is that is carrying the action of the verbs of salvation. It is always the Lord. And that's good news!

19. In recent years, we have witnessed the popularity of books such as *The Purpose-Driven Life* that tend to emphasize the Christian life as a life that is lived by conformity to biblical principles. How are the Law and the Gospel confused if a person reads the Bible merely as a guide for living?

20. Read Galatians 2:17–21 and Ephesians 2:8–10. How does a reading of Scripture that rightly distinguishes the Law and the Gospel keep the Christian's life of good works focused in Christ and not in oneself?

## The Gospel Predominates

We observed in our study of Romans 3:19–31 that all have sinned and fall short of the glory of God. All have sinned, but sinners come in two varieties. There are secure sinners like the Pharisee in the parable of Luke 18:9–14. He was proud of his own piety and trusted in it. And then there are the broken sinners like the tax collector in the same story. He knew the verdict of the Law all too well.

Luther described the preaching of God's Law and Gospel as His alien and proper work. It's alien work in that it is really foreign to His nature. He takes no delight in crushing sinners and condemning them with His wrath. Yet that is just what His Law does. But He does this alien work so that He can finally do His proper work, the work that God loves to do, namely, forgiving sinners who have been broken by their sin and who look to His mercy, not their own merit. Law and Gospel are both there in the Bible, but the Gospel is the goal. It is God's ultimate Word of forgiveness and peace. You have not finished your study of any biblical text until you get to that Good News.

21. Read Luke 15:11–32. Who is the broken sinner in this story? Who is the secure sinner? Where is the Gospel?

22. Read John 5:39–47. How does this text demonstrate the relationship of the Gospel to the Scriptures?

## Spiritual Exercises

- Spend time each day this week studying and praying the following hymns that are models of proper distinction of the Law and the Gospel:

  S. "Dear Christians, One and All" (*LSB* 556; *CW* 377; *LW* 353; *LBW* 299; *TLH* 387)

  M. "Salvation unto Us Has Come" (*LSB* 555; *CW* 390; *LW* 355; *LBW* 297; *TLH* 377)

  T. "Here Is the Tenfold Sure Command" (*CW* 285; *LW* 331)

  W. "The Law of God Is Good and Wise" (*LSB* 579; *CW* 287; *LW* 329; *TLH* 295)

  T. "The Gospel Shows the Father's Grace" (*LSB* 580; *CW* 288; *LW* 330; *TLH* 297)

  F. "All Mankind Fell in Adam's Fall" (*LSB* 562; *CW* 378; *LW* 363; *TLH* 369)

  S. "I Trust, O Christ, in You Alone" (*CW* 437; *LW* 357; *LBW* 395)

- How might your study of Law and Gospel sharpen your listening to preaching? As you listen to the sermon this coming Sunday, intentionally listen for the distinction of Law and Gospel in your pastor's sermon.

- Pray that God would deepen in you the ability to rightly distinguish the Law and Gospel in the opportunities that He gives you to speak His Word to others in daily life.

# Point to Remember

For I am not ashamed of the gospel, for it is the power of God for salvation to everyone who believes, to the Jew first and also to the Greek. For in it the righteousness of God is revealed from faith for faith, as it is written, "The righteous shall live by faith." Romans 1:16–17

To prepare for "Word and Spirit," read Genesis 3:1–13.

# Word and Spirit

*The Holy Spirit does not do one thing and the Word another in working out God's saving purpose in man; by the same action they perform one work and accomplish one effect, just as the mind and eyes see by one and not by different actions. It is only by virtue of the fact that God is in the Word that this Word has the power to accomplish anything spiritual. The Word is powerless if God is not present in it. Any Word which proceeds from God brings God with it. All this is very important. If the Spirit is separated from the Word of God, it is no longer the Word of God. And because God is always with His Word, the power of the Word is the power of God.*

Robert Preus, *The Inspiration of Scripture*, page 184

Wherever God's Word is there is His Spirit also. The Hebrew word for *breath* and *spirit* is the same. Without breathing there can be no speaking. Words are shaped and carried out of the mouth as we breathe. In Psalm 33:6, we see how the Lord's breath and His Word are held together: "By the word of the LORD the heavens were made, and by the breath of his mouth all their host." So when Jesus promises to send His Spirit, the Spirit of Truth, He ties the Spirit to His Word: "If anyone loves Me, he will keep My word, and My Father will love him, and We will come to him and make Our home with him" (John 15:23). It is the Spirit dispatched by Jesus that brings the disciples to remember all that Jesus said (see John 15:26). Word and Spirit are inseparable. The Word is never Spiritless and the Spirit is never Wordless. Where the one is there is the other also.

23. *Spirituality* is one of the buzz words of our culture. But not everything spiritual may be attributed to the Holy Spirit. Discuss examples of spiritualities that pull God's Word and His Spirit apart. Why is this dangerous?

# Let Not Man Put Asunder

24. Read Genesis 3:1–13. How does the serpent contradict God's Word in verse 4?

25. What is the promise of the serpent's spirituality in verse 5?

26. What does Eve rely on in verse 6?

27. What is the outcome of this deception according to verse 7?

28. How does Eve's spirituality attempt to separate God's Word from the Spirit?

29. In contrast to the tragic account of our first parents in garden, there stands the story of our Lord in the wilderness in Matthew 4:1–11. How does Jesus' use of the Scripture demonstrate the unity of Word and Spirit?

# A Tragic Divorce

Attempting to divide God's Word from His Spirit, means that we, in fact, lose both. We see this in every attempt to pit God's Word against His Spirit. For example, there are those who would assert that while the Scriptures forbid the ordination of women to the pastoral office or condemn homosexual activity, the Holy Spirit has led the church today into a new truth that now makes these practices acceptable. Here the Spirit is not confessed as residing in His Word but moving beyond it. This is what Luther and the Lutheran Confessions identified as Enthusiasm. Commenting on John 16, Luther writes,

> Here Christ makes the Holy Spirit a Preacher. He does so to prevent one from gaping toward heaven in search of Him, as the fluttering spirits and enthusiasts do, and from divorcing Him from the oral Word or the ministry. One should know and learn that He will be in and with the Word, that it will guide us into all truth, in order that we may believe it, use it as a weapon, be preserved by it against all the lies and deception of the devil, and prevail in all trials and temptations. . . . The Holy Spirit wants this truth which He is to impress into our hearts to be so firmly fixed that reason and all one's own thoughts and feelings are relegated to the background. He wants us to adhere solely to the Word and to regard it as the only truth. And through this Word alone He governs the Christian Church to the end. (AE 24:362)

30. Read Galatians 1:6–9. Why does Paul condemn the Galatians' version of Enthusiasm so strongly?

31. What happens when Christians forsake the Holy Scriptures as the Spirit's Word? Read 1 Timothy 4:4. Where is this happening today?

# The Word Works

Because God's Word is filled with His Spirit, it is never static but living and working God's own purposes. God's Word says what it does and does what it says. Alive with God's Spirit, His Word bestows what it promises. It does not merely describe who Christ is and what He does as our Savior; it delivers Him to us, creating faith, which receives Him. The knowledge that God's Word is potent enlivens in us patience to hear and speak His Word with confidence, knowing that it will accomplish His will.

32. Read Isaiah 55:8–11. How does Isaiah demonstrate the connectedness between Word and Spirit? Also see Jeremiah 1:11–12 and 23:29.

33. Read Hebrews 4:12–16. What does God's Word do? How does this text shape our use of God's Word?

# Spiritual Exercises

- This week, meditate on Luther's explanation to the Second Petition in the Small Catechism. Notice especially the way the Spirit and the Word are linked together as we confess: "God's kingdom comes when our heavenly Father gives us His Holy Spirit, so that by His grace we believe His holy Word and lead godly lives here in time and there in eternity."
- Study the hymn "O Morning Star, How Fair and Bright" (*LSB* 395; *LW* 73; *LBW* 76). How does this hymn confess the unity of Word and Spirit and the gifts that Christ bestows on us therein?
- Pray this week for all preachers and hearers of the Word of the Lord, asking God to strengthen those who proclaim His Word in the truth and that those who hear it might, through His Spirit, trust Him in life and in death.

# Point to Remember

It is the Spirit who gives life; the flesh is of no avail. The words that I have spoken to you are spirit and life. John 6:63

To prepare for "Inwardly Digesting the Word," read Psalms 1 and 119:97–104.

03

# Inwardly Digesting the Word

*Secondly, you should meditate, that is, not only in your heart, but also externally, by actually repeating and comparing oral speech and literal words of the book, reading and re-reading them with diligent attention and reflection, so that you may see what the Holy Spirit means by them. And take care that you do not grow weary or think that you have done enough when you have read, heard, and spoken them once or twice, and that you then have complete understanding. . . . Thus you see in this same Psalm [Psalm 119] how David constantly boasts that he will talk, meditate, speak, sing, hear, read, by day and night and always, about nothing except God's Word and commandments. For God will not give you His Spirit without the external Word; so take your cue from that.*

Martin Luther, AE 34:286

The words of an old collect ask God to bless our use of His Scriptures so that we may "read, mark, learn and inwardly digest them, that by the patience and comfort" of His Word we may embrace and ever hold fast the gift of eternal life. To meditate on God's Word is to let that Word reside in heart and mind. It is to be at home in the Scriptures and to let the Scriptures be at home in you, so that your mind is formed by their truth and your tongue is untied to declare the redeeming work of our Savior. Luther, in his usual graphic way, compares meditation to a cow chewing its cud. He does this in his commentary on Deuteronomy 14:1 where he states, "To chew the cud, however, is to take up the Word with delight and meditate with supreme diligence, so that (according to the proverb) one does not permit it to go into one ear and out the other, but holds it firmly in the heart, swallows it, and absorbs it into the intestines" (AE 9:136).

34. What do you think of when you hear the word *meditation*? What makes Christian meditation unique?

## Continuing in Jesus' Word

35. Read Psalm 1. What is the basic contrast portrayed in this psalm?

36. Where is the delight of the blessed man according to verse 2? Compare this verse with Psalm 119:33–48.

37. How does the psalmist describe the scope of the blessed man's mediation?

38. What are the results of this meditation?

39. How are unbelievers characterized in this psalm?

40. What light does John 15:1–11 shed on this psalm?

# Chewing on the Word

In Psalm 119:103, David extols the sweetness of God's Word. Deuteronomy 8:3 speaks of how God fed His people manna in the wilderness declaring that "man does not live by bread alone, but man lives by every word that comes from the mouth of the LORD." This verse is quoted by Jesus against the tempter in Matthew 4:4. Ezekiel is commanded to take the scroll and eat it. When he does, it is as sweet as honey to his taste (see Ezekiel 3:1).

41. Why is it that the Scriptures often speak of our feeding on God's Word?

42. How to we devour the Word?

# Strengthened for Life in the World

To meditate on God's Word is to cherish it, to cling to it as our dearest treasure in life and death. Nourished by the Word, we are built up in faith and set free for a life of love toward the neighbor.

43. Read John 8:31–36. What is the relationship between the truth of Jesus' Word and freedom?

44. Read John 17:6–17. What does Jesus promise about His Word?

# Spiritual Exercises

- In his open letter to his barber, Luther suggested a simple way to meditate on God's Word. He advised that Peter the barber take each commandment (or another text from the Scripture) "in their fourfold aspect, namely as a school text, song book, penitential book, and prayer book" (AE 43:209). In other words, Luther advises that four questions be put to the text: What am I taught about God? For what should I give Him thanks? What sins are uncovered that I should confess? What does this text teach me to pray for? Over the next ten days, take each of the Ten Commandments, one a day, and apply Luther's questions, using them as a school book, song book, penitential book, and prayer book.

- In his Genesis lectures, Luther wrote,

  Let him who wants to contemplate in the right way reflect on his Baptism; let him read his Bible, hear sermons, honor father and mother, and come to the aid of a brother in distress. But let him not shut himself up in a nook . . . and there entertain himself with his devotions and thus suppose that he is sitting in God's bosom and has fellowship with God without Christ, without the Word, without the sacraments. (AE 3:275)

  How does Luther's advice keep you both in the Word and the world?

- In 1521, Luther wrote a little guide for Bible study entitled "A Brief Instruction on What to Look for and Expect in the Gospels." In this tract, he said,

  When you open the book containing the gospels and read or hear how Christ comes here or there, or how someone is brought to Him, you should therein perceive the sermon or the gospel through which He is coming to you, or you are being brought to Him. For the preaching of the gospel is nothing else than Christ coming to us, or we being brought to Him. When you see how He works, however, and how He helps everyone to whom He comes or who is brought to Him, then rest assured that faith is accomplishing this in you and that He is offering your soul exactly the same sort of help and favor through the gospel. If you pause here and let Him do you good, that is, if you believe that He benefits and helps you, then you really have it. Then Christ is yours, presented to you as a gift. (AE 35:121)

Try Luther's advice out as you hear the Holy Gospel read in church next Sunday.

## Point to Remember

Sanctify them in the truth; your word is truth. John 17:17

To prepare for "Praying the Word," read John 16:12–24.

# Praying the Word

*The richness of the Word of God ought to determine our prayer, not the poverty of our heart.*

Dietrich Bonhoeffer, *Psalms: The Prayer Book of the Bible,* page 15

Prayer is the voice of faith and faith comes by the hearing of God's Word. He speaks His Word, which creates and sustains faith. The strong Word of the Gospel unlocks lips to call upon God in prayer and thanksgiving. God even gives us words to pray as we see in the Psalms and the Lord's Prayer. His Word sets the agenda for our praying. Adolph Köberle, a Lutheran theologian of the last century, wisely counsels:

> Prayer escapes the danger of disorder and confusion only when it is enkindled by the words of Scripture. From the Word proceeds its inner justification, as well as its life-giving power and the clearness of its petitions. A prayer that does not stick to Scripture will soon become poor in ideas, poor in faith, poor in love, and will finally die. (*The Quest for Holiness*, 176–77)

45. How does God's Word give certainty to our praying?

## A Command and Promise

46. Read John 16:12–24. How does Jesus speak of His relationship to the Father and the Spirit in verses 12–16?

47. On whose authority does the Spirit speak? What does this tell us about the inspiration and authority of the Scriptures?

48. Where does the Spirit take what belongs to Jesus and declare it to us?

49. Jesus speaks the words of our text as part of His farewell discourse to His apostles on the night of His betrayal. What do the apostles receive? Also see 1 John 1:1–4.

50. How is praying in Jesus' name (John 16:23) connected with the Scriptures?

51. According to John 16:24, what is the outcome of such prayer?

## Seeking God's Face

Read Psalm 27:8–9. In Jesus Christ, God's Fatherly heart is revealed. We do not worship a nameless deity or an unknown God. God is never generic. The true God has revealed Himself to us in the Word made flesh, and it is to Him that the Scriptures testify. Because they are the Word of the Lord, who does not lie or deceive, we rightly speak of their inerrancy and infallibility. In the Scriptures,

God invites us to seek His face and it is from the Scriptures that He causes His face to shine upon us with favor.

52. Read John 14:1–11. What does Philip request of Jesus? How does Jesus answer Philip?

53. What does this conversation between Jesus and Philip teach us about the reading of Scripture?

## The Gift of Certainty

At the end of his explanation of each article of the Creed in the Catechism, Luther confesses, "This is most certainly true." God is at work in His Scriptures to dispel the fog of doubt and uncertainty so that we lay hold of His promises with faith. The certainty is not in us but in the steadfast works of God. If God does it, you can be certain that it is done. He inspired the Scriptures, using His eye and ear witnesses to proclaim to us the truth of Jesus' incarnation, death, and resurrection for us. They are not "cleverly devised myths" generated by human impulse. They are the Word of God. The clarity and efficacy of the Holy Scriptures give us the certainty of our salvation. That gives us boldness and confidence in believing and in praying.

54. After the Scripture is read in the Divine Service, the pastor usually says "This is the Word of the Lord" and the congregation responds, "Thanks be to God." How does this liturgical practice confess the authority of Scripture?

55. Sometimes it is argued that the Bible is a complex book, open to multiple interpretations, its words easily twisted, so that no one reading can be correct. Thus, this argument states, we are left with uncertainty as to what God actually says. Review 2 Peter

1:19–21. How would you answer this objection to the clarity of the Scripture?

## Spiritual Exercises

- Luther writes: "Hence it is that the Psalter is the book of all saints; and everyone, in whatever situation he may be, finds in that situation psalms and words that fit his case, that suit him as if they were put there just for his sake, so that he could not put it better himself, or find or wish for anything better" (AE 35:256). Begin and end each day this week with the praying of a psalm. In the morning, pray Psalm 3 and in the evening pray Psalm 4.
- The Lord's Prayer is both God's words to us and our words to God. It is a template for all our praying. Prepare your personal list of intercessions and thanksgiving using the Lord's Prayer as a guide.
- The Lord's Prayer and the Book of Psalms interpenetrate each other. Identity one psalm that best exemplifies each petition of the Lord's Prayer. How does this psalm deepen your praying of the Lord's Prayer?

## Point to Remember

O Lord, open my lips, and mouth will declare your praise. Psalm 51:15

To prepare for "The Comfort of the Word," read Romans 15:4–13.

# The Comfort of the Word

*Firstly, you should know that the Holy Scripture's constitute
a book which turns the wisdom of all other books into foolishness, because not one teaches about eternal life except this
one alone. Therefore you should straightway despair of your
reason and understanding. With them you will not attain
eternal life, but, on the contrary, your presumptuousness will
plunge you and others with you out of heaven (as happened
to Lucifer) into the abyss of hell. But kneel down in your little room [Matthew 6:6] and pray to God with real humility
and earnestness, that He through His dear Son may give you
his Holy Spirit, who will enlighten you, lead you, and give
you understanding.*

Martin Luther, AE 34:285

Contrary to folk wisdom, the conscience is not a reliable guide.
Scared with the memory of sin, it accuses and condemns, or it seeks
to suppress the knowledge of sin by excusing sinfulness with eager
self-justifications. God's Scriptures were written to bring consolation
to consciences terrorized by sin. We exercise ourselves in Holy Scripture so that we might draw on God's comfort for our own distressed
souls. Having thus been comforted, we are able to speak the Lord's
words of consolation to others. So Luther writes,

> Therefore I admonish you, especially those of you who
> are to become instructors of consciences, as well as each
> of you individually, that you exercise yourselves by study,
> by reading, by meditation, and by prayer, so that in temp-
> tation you will be able to instruct consciences, both your
> own and others, console them, and take them from the
> Law to grace, from active righteousness to passive right-
> eousness, in short, from Moses to Christ. In affliction and
> in the conflict of conscience it is the devil's habit to
> frighten us with the Law and to set against us the con-
> sciousness of sin, our wicked past, the wrath and judg-

ment of God, hell and eternal death, so that thus he may drive us into despair, subject us to himself, and pluck us from Christ. (AE 26:10)

56. Can you recount episodes in your own dealing with people or from the media where conscience has been allowed to take priority over God's Word?

# Written For You

57. Read Romans 15:4–13. According to verse 4, why was the Old Testament written? How does this shape the way we read it?

58. Paul writes of endurance and encouragement in verse 4 and then he repeats these two words in verse 5. What is the significance of these two words? Also see James 1:2–18.

59. What is the outcome of the Scriptures' use in Romans 15:4?

60. According to verse 8, how did Christ confirm God's truthfulness?

61. What is Paul doing by citing a string of Old Testament passages in verses 9–12?

62. How does Romans 15:4–13 reflect the connection between God's Word and His Holy Spirit?

# Light in the Darkness

We find comfort in the Scriptures because they are clear. The clarity of the Scriptures is in Christ Jesus, who is the "light of the world" (John 8:12). He is the light that shines in the darkness and is not overcome by it (see John 1:4–5). By His Gospel, He has called us out of darkness into his marvelous light (see 1 Peter 2:9 and 2 Corinthians 4:6). And in His light we see light (Psalm 36:9). The Scriptures shine clear and pure with the radiance of their Lord so that the Psalmist testifies "Your word is a lamp to my feet and a light to my path" (Psalm 119:105). The apostle Peter echoes this as he writes that we have the sureness of the prophetic word shining as a lamp in a dark place (see 2 Peter 1:19). The Scriptures do not leave us with a hidden God (*deus absconditus*) but God revealed in Christ (*deus revelatus*).

63. How do readings of Scripture that would subject them to human reason, tradition, or experience obscure both the essential clarity of the Bible and the comfort that God would give us in Christ?

64. Mark Twain once quipped that what troubled him about the Bible was not those passages that were unclear or beyond his understanding but those clear passages that he understood all too well. What do arguments that Scripture is unclear often reveal about the interpreter?

# Words to Speak

We study the Scriptures not to become better Bible trivia players but so that God's Word will dwell in us richly. We hear the reading and the preaching of Scriptures that we might be strengthened in our faith in Jesus Christ. We read the Bible so that we might be comforted in the forgiveness of sins and enlivened in the hope of life eternal. Our ears and hearts are filled with the Word of God so that we might also speak it to both our fellow-believers and to those who are still in the darkness of unbelief. Also see Colossians 3:16–17.

65. Read 2 Corinthians 1:3–7. How does your reading and hearing of the Scriptures both comfort you and enable you to comfort others?

66. Read 1 Peter 3:15. How are Christians prepared to give an answer for their hope in Christ?

## Spiritual Exercises

- Martin Luther complied a list of Bible passages called "Sayings in Which Luther Found Comfort" (AE 43:171–77). Start a journal of biblical texts that you find especially comforting.
- Pray your way through Psalm 119, marking all the places that speak of God's Word as giving light, guidance, and comfort.
- Learn by heart the hymn, "God's Word Is Our Great Heritage" (*LSB* 582; *CW* 293; *LW* 333; *LBW* 239; *TLH* 283) or "Lord, Keep Us Steadfast in Your Word" (*LSB* 655; *CW* 203; *LW* 334; *LBW* 230; *TLH* 261).

## Point to Remember

Heaven and earth will pass away, but My words will not pass away. Matthew 24:35

# Leader Guide

Leaders, please note the different abilities of your Bible study participants. Some will easily find the many passages listed in this study. Others will struggle to find even the "easy" passages. To help everyone participate, team up members of the class. For example, if a question asks you to look up several passages, assign one passage to one group, the second to another, and so on. Divide up the work! Let participants present the different answers they discover.

Each topic is divided into four easy-to-use sections.

**Focus** introduces participants to key concepts that will be discovered in the session.

**Inform** guides participants into Scripture to uncover biblical truth.

**Connect** enables participants to apply that which is learned in Scripture to their lives.

**Vision** provides participants with practical suggestions for extending the theme of the lesson out of the classroom and into the world.

# The God Who Speaks

## Objectives

By the power of the Holy Spirit working through God's Word, participants will (1) see the connection between the Word made flesh, our Lord Jesus Christ and the Holy Scriptures as they testify to Him and His saving work of the justification of the ungodly by faith alone; (2) see the connection between the Scriptures and the Christian sermon and grow in their ability to hear preaching as the living voice of Christ Jesus; and (3) respond in the development of a regular pattern of the study of Holy Scripture in light of weekly worship with the congregation gathered around preaching and the Lord's Supper.

## Opening Worship

O God, in the glorious transfiguration of Your only-begotten Son, You once confirmed the mysteries of the faith by the testimonies of the ancient fathers, and in the voice that came from the bright cloud You wondrously foreshowed our adoption by grace. Therefore, mercifully make us co-heirs with our King of His glory, and bring us to the fullness of our inheritance in heaven; through Jesus Christ, our Lord, who lives and reigns with You and the Holy Spirit, one God, now and forever. Amen.

Sing "Speak, O Lord, Your Servant Listens" (*LSB* 589; *ELH* 230; *CW* 283; *LW* 339; *TLH* 296).

## Focus

1. Answers may vary. For some it may be a perceived lack of time. For others it may be boredom or a lack of discipline. At this point, the leader may desire to direct participants to the parable of the sower (Matthew 13:1–9, 18–23), pointing out how Satan, the world, and our sinful flesh obstruct the hearing of God's Word. The leader may also refer to the story of Mary and Martha (see Luke 10:38–42).

# By the Prophets

2. In the Old Testament, God spoke to His people in a variety of ways including visions (Genesis 15:1), the burning bush (Exodus 3:1–12), and a low whisper (1 Kings 19:9–18). In other instances, such as Genesis 12:1–3, we are simply told that God spoke or that the Word of the Lord came to the prophet (Jeremiah 1:1–10).

3. Samuel answers the Lord's call: "Speak, for your servant hears" (1 Samuel 13:10).

4. God speaks to us now in His Son. He is God's ultimate Word to us. We do not rely on dreams or charismatic experiences to discover God's will for our lives. We listen to the Son, who speaks to us in and through His Gospel. No matter how spiritual the experience may seem or angelic the messenger may appear, if it contradicts the Gospel, it is to be rejected (see Galatians 1:8). The following words from Luther demonstrate how seriously Luther took this truth:

> Christ once appeared visible here on earth and showed his glory, and according to the divine purpose of God finished the work of redemption and deliverance of mankind. I do not desire He should come to me once more in the same manner, neither would I He should send an angel unto me. Nay, though an angel should appear before mine eyes from heaven, yet it would not add to my belief; for I have of my Saviour Christ Jesus bond and seal; I have His Word, Spirit, and sacrament; thereon I depend, and desire no new revelations. And the more steadfastly to confirm me in this resolution, to hold solely to God's Word, and not to give credit to any visions or revelations, I shall relate the following circumstance: —On Good Friday last, I being in my chamber in fervent prayer, contemplating with myself, how Christ my Saviour on the cross suffered and died for our sins, there suddenly appeared on the wall a bright vision of our Saviour Christ, with the five wounds, steadfastly looking upon me, as if had been Christ himself corporeally. At first sight, I thought it had been some celestial revelation, but I reflected that it must needs be an illusion and juggling of the devil, for Christ appeared to us in His Word, and in a meaner and more humble form; therefore I spake to the vision thus: Avoid thee, confounded devil: I know no

other Christ than He who was crucified, and who in His Word is pictured and presented unto me. Whereupon the image vanished, clearly showing of whom it came. (Hugh T. Kerr's *A Compend of Luther's Theology,* p. 57)

5. The Old Testament indicates that it was necessary that Christ should suffer and on the third day rise from the dead and that repentance and forgiveness of sins should be preached in his name to all the nations beginning in Jerusalem. Also see Acts 10:43.

6. Hebrews 1:2 describes God's Son as the heir of all things and the One through whom the Father created the world. Also see John 1:2–3 and Colossians 1:15–17.

7. God created all things through the eternal Word, who is His Son, Jesus.

## Listening to the Son

8. Moses represents the Law and Elijah signifies the prophets. In other words, the Law and the Prophets testify to Jesus. They speak to Him about "His departure, which He was about to accomplish at Jerusalem" (Luke 9:31). The Greek word used for "departure" is *exodon* ("exodus"), thus recalling the Old Testament deliverance of Israel from Egypt with the death of the Passover Lamb (see Exodus 12).

9. In this passage, the apostle links the inspiration of Scripture to the incarnation of the Son of God. The apostles, who are the eye and ear witnesses (see 1 John 1:1–4) of the coming of our Lord, testify to His reality. This is not mythology, but factual history in time and space. The apostles testify to the glory of God made manifest in the humanity of Jesus. The Scriptures are to be interpreted in light of their origin. Interpretation is not left to the imagination of the reader because the Scriptures were not the product of human impulses, but Spirit-sent from the Father through the Son.

## Where Do We Hear God?

10. The ordering of these readings move from the Old Testament (prophet) to the Epistle (letter of an apostle) to the Holy Gospel (evangelist) to the sermon (preached by the pastor; see Ephesians 4:11). The proclaimed Word of the sermon is based on and governed by the written Word of Holy Scripture. Peter confesses that Jesus has "the words of eternal life" (John 6:68); therefore, we sing these words

in anticipation of the reading of the Holy Gospel in the Divine Service.

11. We are hearing Jesus when we listen to preaching faithful to His Word. Here, the leader may point out how the Lutheran Confessions use this text:

> According to this Gospel authority, as a matter of necessity, by divine right, congregations obey must them, for Luke 10:16, says "The one who hears you hears Me." But when they teach or establish anything against the Gospel, then the congregations are forbidden by God's command to obey them (Augsburg Confession XXVIII 22–23)

and

> Ministers act in Christ's place and do not represent their own persons, according to Luke, "The one who hears you hears Me" (10:16). Ungodly teachers are to be deserted because they no longer act in Christ's place, but are antichrists. Christ says, "Beware of false prophets" (Matthew 7:15). Paul says, "If anyone is preaching to you a gospel contrary to the one you received, let him be accursed" (Galatians 1:9) (Apology of the Augsburg Confession VII/VIII 47–48).

# The Words That Kill
# and Give Life

## Objectives

By the power of the Holy Spirit, working through God's Word, participants will (1) understand the necessity of rightly distinguishing the Law and the Gospel in reading the Holy Scriptures; (2) be able to diagnose confusions of the Law and the Gospel; and (3) grow in their confidence in the salvation delivered to us in the Gospel alone.

## Opening Worship

Almighty God, our heavenly Father, out of Your tender love towards us sinners You have given us Your Son, that, believing in Him, we might have everlasting life. Continue to grant us Your Holy Spirit that we may remain steadfast in this faith to the end and come to life everlasting; through Jesus Christ, our Lord. Amen.

Sing "Here Is the Tenfold Sure Command" (*CW* 285; *LW* 331).

## Focus

12. The leader may need to guide the discussion here by presenting a basic description of how God's Law functions to show us our sin, that is our unbelief, which is made manifest in our thoughts, words, and deeds in contrast to the Gospel, which itself bespeaks the forgiveness of sins. The distinction is made difficult because the old Adam clings to what Luther called the *opinio legis,* that is, the inborn "opinion of the law," that human efforts must in some manner contribute to salvation. When human beings take God's Law in hand, it is natural that its use ends up either in despair or self-righteousness. The Gospel declares not man's righteousness but the righteousness of God. The Law is all about man and his sin. The Gospel is all about God and the redemption He has won for the world in the blood of Jesus. The Gospel declares pardon to the guilty, righteousness for the unrighteous, and life for those who are dead in sin. For additional help with this distinction, note the excerpts from Article V in the

Formula of Concord included on p. 60 in this book or see *Handling the Word of Truth: Law and Gospel in the Church Today* by John T. Pless (CPH, 2004).

# A Life and Death Distinction

13. The Law speaks to all people, for all have sinned. It condemns the Jews for they were given the Law in written form in the Decalogue transmitted through Moses at Mt. Sinai. The Gentiles may not plead exemption from the Law because God has written it in their hearts. All are held accountable by God's Law.

14. The Law lacks the power to save. It is impotent to give sinners righteousness before God. The Law gives us the knowledge of our sinfulness. Here, the leader may refer participants to the words of stanza 3 of the great Reformation hymn, "Salvation unto Us Has Come" for its succinct definition: "It was a false, misleading dream That God his Law had given That sinners could themselves redeem And by their works gain heaven. The Law is but a mirror bright To bring the inbred sin to light That lurks within our nature" (*LW* 355).

15. The righteousness of God is His redeeming work to save sinners accomplished by His Son, who has reconciled us to God by taking our sin upon Himself and dying in our place. See 2 Corinthians 5:18–21.

16. God justifies sinners through the atoning death of His Son, as Paul states in Romans 3:23–25. All are justified by God's grace as a gift through the redemption that is in Christ Jesus. This gift of salvation is received by faith alone. Faith receives the gift.

17. In Romans 3:27, the apostle writes that our boasting is excluded on the basis of faith. Faith is not a human work, but the work of God through His Word. It renders us passive in the sense that we have contributed nothing to our salvation. It is a gift. Thus, all human boasting of merit or effort is excluded.

18. Justification by faith alone does not overthrow the Law so that we become lawless (antinomianism) or so that we "continue in sin that grace may abound" (see Romans 6:1). Rather the Law finds its proper end or goal in Christ: "For Christ is the end of the law for righteousness to everyone who believes" (Romans 10:4). The condemnation of the Law is answered in Christ alone for He is our Righteousness. Living by faith in Him we are freed from condemnation (see Romans 8:1) even as the Law continues to put to death the

old man who still lives within us, uncovering and convicting us of every impulse to walk by the flesh rather than the Spirit. Thus, justification by faith alone does not overthrow the Law but confirms the Law's verdict of our sinfulness. Since Christians are at one and the same time both saint and sinner (*simul iustus et peccator*), the Law cannot be dismissed, but remains in place to put to death all that is not of Christ and to guide us away from self-chosen good works that tempt us to establish our own righteousness apart from faith in Jesus.

## To Mix Is to Muddle

19. Give participants an opportunity to reflect on books and programs that see the Christian life in terms of principles for sanctified living or the Bible as a "How-to" manual. Draw the contrast with the Scriptures' portrayal of the Christian life as a life that is lived by faith. Direct participants to Colossians 2:6–7. Here, point out the confusion of the Law and the Gospel in *The Purpose-Driven Life*. The author, Rick Warren, asserts that "The smile of God is the goal of your life. Since pleasing God is the first purpose of your life, your most important task is to discover how to do that" (Rick Warren, *The Purpose-Driven Life* [Grand Rapids, MI: Zondervan, 2002], p. 69). Contrary to Warren, God does not smile on us because of our obedience or good works, but solely on account of what Jesus has done for us. Here the comments of the Australian Lutheran theologian John Strelan are to the point:

> Once again, the distortion is deadly for the troubled conscience. The gospel announces: for Christ's sake, because of Christ, God forgives us, is merciful to us, smiles on us. Christians pray with the psalmist, "Smile on us and save us" (Psalm 80:19). When God looks at us, he sees Christ and his righteousness—and he smiles on us. God's smile is the sun which brings to life in us the love and trust and obedience and praise and service of God which pleases [H]im so. . . . God smiles on us, and that smile enables us to love and trust and obey and serve [H]im. The legalized "gospel" says: when/if we do these things, then God smiles on us. This is a saddening exchange of law for gospel. It fails to magnify Christ and it fails to comfort troubled sinners. (John Strelan, "The Legalization of the Gospel," *Lutheran Theological Journal,* August/December 2005, p. 129)

20. Both of these texts speak of the life that is lived in Christ by faith. Good works have absolutely nothing to contribute to salvation. Good works are a fruit of faith. They are not offered to God as an attempt to satisfy Him but they are directed to the need of the neighbor. God does need our good works, but our neighbor does. We insult God when we attempt to drag our piety and works into heaven. God is honored most when we cling to His promises by faith and, set free from every attempt to make ourselves righteous, we focus on the good works that God has prepared beforehand, works defined by His commandments and directed toward the well-being of our neighbor.

## The Gospel Predominates

21. That all have sinned and fall short of the glory of God is the truth we hear in Romans 3. But sinners come in two varieties. There are sinners who recognize their sin and are broken by it like the prodigal son in the familiar parable of Luke 15. Then there are sinners like the older son, who is secure in the knowledge that he had lived a life of obedience to his father. The younger son sins in his rebellion, his attempt to live life on his own terms apart from his father's house. The older son sins in his self righteousness. The Gospel in the parable is found in the father who humiliates himself to embrace and reclaim the son whose life was broken by the Law. You may also wish to look at two other examples of broken and secure sinners in Luke's Gospel—the story of the Pharisee and the tax collector (18:9–14) and the account of the two thieves crucified with Jesus (Luke 23:39–43).

22. To refuse to hear the Scriptures is to refuse to hear Jesus. The Jews had Moses (the Law) and claimed allegiance to the Old Testament—yet in their refusal to believe Jesus, they stand accused by their own Scriptures.

# Word and Spirit

## Objectives

By the power of the Holy Spirit working through God's Word, participants will (1) see that God's Word bears His Holy Spirit so that when they hear His Word they will be confident that it is God Himself speaking; (2) be equipped to respond from the Scriptures to religious groups that seek the Spirit apart from the Word; and (3) rejoice in the efficacy of God's Word and trust in it to do what the Lord has promised.

## Opening Worship

Almighty God, grant to Your Church Your Holy Spirit and the wisdom that comes down from heaven, that Your Word may not be bound, but have free course and be preached to the joy and edifying of Christ's holy people, that in steadfast faith we may serve You and in the confession of Your name may abide to the end; through Jesus Christ, our Lord. Amen.

Sing "God Has Spoken by His Prophets" (*LSB* 583; *CW* 281; *LW* 343; *LBW* 238).

## Focus

23. Spirituality comes in a variety of shapes and forms. More often than not, the word is used to refer to anything that is vaguely religious. Participants might mention such things as the New Age Movement, Eastern religions, or American civil religion with its generic and inclusive descriptions of the deity. It is important for participants to understand that not all talk of spirituality is of the Holy Spirit. Spirituality leaves us with the hidden God, a deity of our own imagination. We know the Holy Spirit only in Christ who is revealed in the Scriptures. Mark Twain said, "In the beginning, God created man in His own image and ever since, man has returned the compliment." Faith relies not on imaginative efforts to reshape God in our own image, but in the true God, who has made Himself known in Jesus Christ. The leader may want to point out that the historical-

45

critical method of studying the Bible questions the reliability of the biblical Gospels. This yields a "Christ of faith," who is not the same as the "historical Jesus." For a brief but thoughtful response to this approach, see Craig Parton's *The Defense Never Rests: A Lawyer's Quest for the Gospel* (CPH, 2003, pp. 49–96). The issue of postmodernism and pluralism might surface in this discussion. For those who want to explore the impact of postmodernism on the interpretation of the Bible, *Above All Earthly Pow'rs: Christ in a Postmodern World*, published by Eerdmans in 2005, is an excellent and reliable guide.

## Let No Man Put Asunder

24. The serpent makes God out to be a liar by contradicting His Word.

25. Here the serpent promises Eve that she will be like God, knowing good and evil as her eyes will behold a vision of something that was beyond her comprehension.

26. Eve relies on what she can see with her eyes rather than the Word that God had spoken. Sight is deemed more real than hearing.

27. The eyes of Adam and Eve were indeed opened, but they see themselves, not God. They see themselves as naked, and in their shame, they try to hide themselves.

28. Eve's spirituality is a sensual spirituality in that it relies on her own sense rather than what God had given her in His Word. She is no longer content to live under God's pronouncement that His creation is "very good" (see Genesis 1:31). The tempter seduces her into the false belief that being like God is superior to being a creature who lives trusting God's Word. For Eve, the Spirit is not to be found in the Word but in having her eyes opened by eating the fruit forbidden by God.

29. Jesus relies on the written Word of God and uses it as weaponry against Satan.

## A Tragic Divorce

30. At this point the leader may wish to refer to Luther's description of *Enthusiasm* in the Smalcald Articles, where he states that the old serpent led Adam and Eve "away from God's outward Word to spiritualizing and self-pride" (Smalcald Articles III VIII 5). Enthusiasm leads away from the real Jesus to a false Christ, who is no Savior

at all. This is the point of Paul's harsh condemnation of the Galatians.

31. When Christians turn away from the Scriptures as God's Word, they become captivated by teachers of their own choosing, who satisfy their spiritual cravings by telling them what they want to hear. In short, they get a deity who is domesticated to their own desires and who affirms them in their personal notions of who God is and how He ought to act.

Answers may vary.

## The Word Works

32. God's Word comes from the Lord's mouth and it accomplishes the purpose for which He sends it. God's Spirit (His breath) is in His speaking. Jeremiah says that God is watching over His Word to perform it (1:11–12) and that God's Word is like a hammer (23:29). God's Word is efficacious as it does what the Lord wills it to do.

33. Hebrews 4:11–12 tells us that God's Word is living and active, sharper than a sword with its ability to penetrate the soul. As we have observed early on in this course, it is really the Scriptures that interpret our lives because we stand under their authority. We do not conform the Scriptures to our notions of truth and rationality, but we are conformed to them as God's Law and Gospel work.

# Inwardly Digesting the Word

## Objectives

By the power of the Holy Spirit working through God's Word, participants will (1) see the value of meditating on the Scriptures; (2) learn to distinguish between evangelical meditation, that is, clinging to the external Word in faith, from various forms of mysticism; and (3) deepen their ability for prayerful study of the Scriptures.

## Opening Worship

Blessed Lord, who has caused the Holy Bible to be written for our learning, grant that we may hear, read, mark, learn, and inwardly digest Your Word, that by patience and the comfort of Thy Holy Scriptures we may embrace, and ever hold fast, the blessed hope of everlasting life, which You have given us in our Savior, Jesus Christ, who lives and reigns with You and the Holy Spirit, ever one God, world without end. Amen.

Sing "Lord, Keep Us Steadfast in Your Word" (*LSB* 655; *ELH* 589; *CW* 203; *LW* 334; *LBW* 230; *TLH* 261).

## Focus

34. Answers may vary. For example, some participants may mention practices associated with mysticism that attempt to clear the soul of earthly concerns so that one may enter into a purified communion with the divine. Others might think of quiet time spent in contemplation or reflection. Christian meditation is not an introspective dwelling on self nor is it an attempt to transcend time and space by way of some mystical technique. Rather, the Christian is like the Virgin Mary, who pondered the Word of God in her heart (see Luke 2:19). Christian meditation is attentiveness to the Word of God read and heard.

# Continuing in Jesus' Word

35. The basic contrast in Psalm 1 is between the righteous and the wicked, between believers and unbelievers. Believers are compared to sturdy and fruitful trees with roots that are refreshed by streams of living water. They do not wither in the heat of a summer drought, but produce fruit in season. On the other hand, unbelievers are like husks blown away by the breeze.

36. The blessed man delights in God's Torah. English translations often render *Torah* as *Law*, but it is essential to remember that the Torah contains both Law and Gospel, so verse 2 is really speaking of God's Word. In many ways Psalm 119:33–48 is an extended commentary on Psalm 1:2. Note especially that the psalmist implores God to teach, guide, preserve, and confirm him in His Word. These verses also speak of meditation (v. 48) and delight in God's Word (vv. 35 and 47). This meditation on God's Word is set in contrast with those who meditate, that is, set their hearts and eyes on worthless things (vv. 36–37).

37. Psalm 1 speaks of the scope of the blessed man's meditation in regard to both time and space. God's Word is continually occupying his heart both day and night. The blessed man does not walk in the way of wickedness but stands in the company of God's people, who are righteous through faith in the Messiah.

38. Rooted and grounded in God's Word, the blessed man bears the fruits of faith even as a well-watered tree is abundant with good fruit. You may direct participants to cross reference Psalm 1:3 with Jeremiah 17:8. Also note Luke 6:43–45 for a New Testament parallel to this text.

39. Unbelievers will not abide in the Lord's presence. They stand under His judgment and without faith they perish.

40. It is only through faith in Jesus that our lives are fruitful. In John 15, Jesus speaks of Himself as the vine and us as the branches. His words live in us and keep us connected to Him by faith and such faith bears fruit that remains.

# Chewing on the Word

41. Without food, there is starvation as the body is deprived and depleted of nourishment. Without the bread of God's Word we would perish spiritually. Even as God opens His hands to satisfy us with daily bread for the body, He also gives us His words, that we

might be satisfied with the gifts of forgiveness of sins, peace with Him, and the sure hope of eternal life. Therefore Jesus says, "Blessed . . . are those who hear the Word of God and keep it" (Luke 11:28).

42. We devour God's Word by "inwardly digesting" it as the earlier collect puts it. We hear it over and over again like a cow chewing her cud, to paraphrase Luther. Faith holds fast to God's Word and digests every particle for the gifts that God has put there to nourish us in faith and love.

## Strengthened for Life in the World

43. Captivity to the Word actually means freedom. Freedom is not to be had apart from God's Word. That would be slavery, bondage to sin. God's Word sets us free. This freedom is not only a freedom from sin, death, and hell; it is a freedom for a life of faith in Christ and love for our neighbor. God's Word is the truth that sets us free.

44. Jesus has made God's name manifest to His disciples. With the Lord's name, He gives us His words, and in these words we know the truth that Jesus is the Son sent from the Father to redeem us by His blood and to sanctify us for a life with Him. In this section of Jesus' high priestly prayer, He intercedes for us in face of the fact that Christians will be hated and persecuted because they have and confess God's Word. Here the leader may guide the group in discussing examples of Christians being accused and persecuted for being intolerant because they refuse to compromise the teaching of God's Word.

# Praying the Word

## Objectives

By the power of the Holy Spirit working through God's Word, participants will (1) see the importance of letting God's Word shape and direct their prayers so that prayer is grounded in the certainty of faith; (2) grow in their appreciation for the psalms in the Christian prayer life; and (3) respond to God's Word in prayer and thanksgiving.

## Opening Worship

Almighty God, since You have granted us the favor to call on You with one accord and have promised that where two or three are gathered together in Your name You are in the midst of them, fulfill now the prayers of Your servants, granting us in this world knowledge of Your truth and life everlasting in the world to come; through Jesus Christ, our Lord. Amen.

Sing "Our Father, Who from Heaven Above" (*LSB* 766; *ELH* 383; *CW* 410; *LW* 431; *TLH* 458).

## Focus

45. Pick up here with the quote from Dietrich Bonhoeffer on page 27. Examine Bonhoeffer's words in light of Jeremiah 17:9 and Matthew 15:19–20. Certainty is not anchored in our hearts, untrustworthy as they are, but in God's Word, which both commands us to pray and promises that those who pray in Jesus' name will be heard. When we pray in Jesus' name we are praying on the basis of who Jesus is (God's Son and our Savior) and all that He has promised us in His name. Direct participants to John 16:23–24. Also note Luther's explanation to both the Introduction and the Conclusion of the Lord's Prayer in the Small Catechism as he speaks of the boldness and confidence that God gives us in His command to pray and the promise to hear us. The certainty that we are given in God's Word is condensed in the single word, *Amen.*

# A Command and Promise

46. Jesus says that all that the Father has is His and that the Spirit will glorify the Son by taking what belongs to Him and declaring it to the apostles.

47. The Spirit speaks not on His own authority, but with the authority of Him who sends Him. Commenting on this section of John 16, Luther writes,

> Here Christ makes the Holy Spirit a Preacher. He does so to prevent one from gaping toward heaven in search of Him, as the fluttering spirits and enthusiasts do, and from divorcing Him from the oral Word or the ministry. One should know and learn that He will be in and with the Word, that it will guide us into all truth, in order that we may believe it, use it as a weapon, be preserved by it against all the lies and deception of the devil, and prevail in all trials and temptations. . . . The Holy Spirit wants this truth which He is to impress into our hearts to be so firmly fixed that reason and all one's own thoughts and feelings are relegated to the background. He wants us to adhere solely to the Word and to regard it as the only truth. And through this Word alone He governs the Christian Church to the end. (AE 24:362)

We have such confidence in the Scriptures because they are inspired by the Spirit of truth.

48. The Spirit is at work in His Word to declare all that Jesus has done for us in coming to be our Savior. Note Luther's comments in the Smalcald Articles: "Therefore, we must constantly maintain this point: God does not want to deal with us in any other way than through the spoken Word and the Sacraments. Whatever is praised as from the Spirit—without the Word and the Sacraments—is the devil himself" (Smalcald Articles III VIII 10).

49. In John 15:26–27, Jesus says that the Spirit of truth, who is sent from the Father, will bear witness to Jesus. He also said that the apostles will bear witness because they have been with Him from the beginning. The apostles bear witness to Jesus because they saw Him with their own eyes, heard Him with their own ears, and touched Him with their own hands (see 1 John 1:1–4; also note Acts 1:2–3 and 1:21–26). In Acts 1:21–26, we observe that the replacement for

Judas had to be a man who was with Jesus from His Baptism to His ascension, and like the other apostles, a witness of His resurrection.

50. All that is given us in Jesus' name is there for us in the Scriptures for "You have exalted above all things Your name and Your word" (Psalm 138:2). To pray in Jesus' name is to pray on the basis of His Word.

51. Here Jesus promises that prayers will be answered and our joy will be made full.

## Seeking God's Face

52. Philip wants to see the Father. Jesus answers Philip by saying that "whoever has seen me has seen the Father" (John 14:9).

53. The conversation between Philip and Jesus comes into play as Luther speaks of the "theology of the cross" in his Heidelberg Theses. Here, Luther observes that Philip wanted to see God, but Jesus pulls him back down to earth so that he sees Jesus. "For this reason true theology and recognition of God are in the crucified Christ" (AE 31:53). Outwardly, Jesus doesn't much look like God, but He is God in the flesh. Outwardly, the Scriptures don't look like what human imagination would envision God's Word to be. But as surely as Jesus is the Son of God, so too the Scriptures are His Word. To see Jesus is to see the Father. To hear or read the Scriptures is to hear or read God's Word.

## The Gift of Certainty

54. In the Divine Service, the Scriptures are read and received not as the words of men but as the very Word of God. Look at 1 Thessalonians 2:13, where Paul gives thanks that the Thessalonians received the apostolic words as the Word of God. This liturgical practice is one way we can publicly acknowledge the authority of the Scriptures.

55. The lack of clarity is not in the Scriptures, but in our own minds, which are blinded by sin. The fact that human beings can and do twist the Scriptures, and ignore or distort God's Word, does not mean that the Scriptures are at fault. It is often the case that people appeal to diversity of interpretations or perceived contradictions in Scripture as a way of attempting to avoid the claim that the Bible makes about God Himself. In other words, the real argument comes down to the First Commandment's divine assertion that we are to have no other gods.

# The Comfort of the Word

## Objectives

By the power of the Holy Spirit working through God's Word, participants will (1) see in the Holy Scriptures the sure promises of God and learn to use these promises for comfort in times of spiritual struggle; (2) rejoice in the clarity of the Scriptures as coming from Christ, the light of the world; and (3) be better equipped to speak God's Word to give peace and hope to those who sit in the darkness of sin.

## Opening Worship

Lord, we thank You that You have taught us what You would have us believe and do. Help us by Your Holy Spirit for the sake of Jesus Christ, to keep Your Word in pure hearts that thereby we may be strengthened in faith, perfected in holiness, and comforted in life and in death. Amen.

Sing "Lord Jesus Christ, With Us Abide" (*LSB* 585; *ELH* 511; *CW* 541; *LW* 344; *TLH* 292).

## Focus

56. Answers may vary. Ultimately the leader will need to make the point that it is God's Word not the human conscience that does not error or deceive.

## Written for You

57. The Old Testament was written to give us hope in the Messiah, whose coming as Savior it promised. The apostle says it was written for our instruction, to teach us how to wait with endurance as we are given encouragement through these Scriptures, which are pregnant with the promises of God.

58. Endurance and encouragement have to do with faith that clings to God when trial and temptation seem to contradict His promises. James 1:2–18 speaks of such testing and the blessing that God

gives even in the midst of life's trials and tests. Luther called these times of testing *tentatio*. As we have noted earlier, Luther describes the *tentatio* as the third part of a triad that includes *oratio* (prayer) and *meditatio* (meditation). Luther says that this *tentatio*:

> is the touchstone which teaches you not only to know and understand, but also to experience how right, how true, how sweet, how lovely, how mighty, how comforting God's Word is, wisdom beyond all wisdom. . . . For as soon as God's Word takes root and grows in you, the devil will harry you, and will make a real doctor of you, and by his assaults will teach you to seek and love God's Word. (AE 34:286–87)

59. The outcome of the Scriptures' use is hope. Hope is faith that is focused toward the future. It does not disappoint because Jesus has been raised from the dead. His future belongs to all who are His by faith (see Romans 5:1–5 and 1 Peter 1:3–9).

60. God confirmed the promises given to the patriarchs by sending His Son, the promised Seed of the woman (Genesis 3:15), who came in the form of a servant (see Philippians 2:7 and Matthew 20:28) to reconcile the world to Himself by the shedding of His blood on the cross.

61. With this sampling of Old Testament texts, Paul is demonstrating that the Gentiles are included in God's promised redemption.

62. The Holy Spirit, who caused the Scriptures to be written in ancient times, is working through those same Scriptures today to give joy and peace in believing (Romans 15:13), and through that faith He causes us to abound in hope.

## Light in the Darkness

63. Our Lutheran Church holds to the *sola scriptura,* that is, the Holy Scriptures alone are the "the pure, clear fountain of Israel. They are the only true standard or norm by which all teachers and doctrines are to be judged" (Formula of Concord, Solid Declaration Summary 3). Human reason, personal experience, and the tradition of the Church are subjected to the normative character of the prophetic and apostolic Scriptures. In one way or another, those who would set reason, experience, or tradition alongside of Scripture argue that the Scripture is either unclear or insufficient. Some will argue that Scripture must be taken as a "conversation partner" in contem-

porary debates on such issues as homosexuality. But when Scripture is reduced to a mere conversation partner, you can be sure that it will not be given the last word. Ultimately, when Scripture is deemed to be lacking either in clarity or sufficiency, struggling sinners are left without the comfort God wills to give us in Jesus.

Here the observation of the German Lutheran theologian Armin Wenz is helpful:

> The *sola Scriptura* principle is derived from the insight discovered in the Scriptures, that there are false traditions, false works, and false exegesis of Scriptures from the beginning of the church. To cut off tradition or to preach against good works *per se* has never been a serious option for the Lutheran Reformation. But the question has and still is: How can we discern true and false doctrine, true and false tradition, true and false works?

> For this reason the *sola Scriptura,* that is, the distinction of Scripture between tradition, is a logical and theological necessity for the sake of the purity of the gospel and for the certainty of salvation for those who put their trust not on their works, or their own ability to understand the Scriptures, but on Christ and His Spirit alone and thereby on His instituted sacraments, including the Scriptures. The *sola Scriptura* therefore is a necessity, as long as we need Christ's Spirit, who promises to create our faith and build the church through these very same means that Christ has instituted for us. It is a necessity as long as we still live in the church militant. (Armin Wenz, "Justification and Holy Scripture," *Logia* XIV, no. 2 [Eastertide 2005]: 12)

64. Such arguments often reveal that the darkness resides not in the Scriptures, but in its detractor. The Scriptures are all too clear about those who live in unbelief. See John 3:36.

## Words to Speak

65. God has comforted us in our afflictions so that we might bring this consolation to others in their sufferings. We read and study the Scriptures so that we might have words to speak to those whose souls are seared with the bitter memory of sin, those whose con-

sciences have been rubbed raw with the accusations of the Law. Luther puts it nicely in his Galatians lectures:

> Therefore I admonish you, especially those of you who are to become instructors of consciences, as well as each of you individually, that you exercise yourselves by study, by reading, by meditation, and by prayer, so that in temptation you will be able to instruct consciences, both your own and others, console them, and take them from the Law to grace, from active righteous to passive righteousness, in short, from Moses to Christ. In affliction and in the conflict of conscience it is the devil's habit to frighten us with the Law and to set against us the consciousness of sin, our wicked past, the wrath and judgment of God, hell and eternal death, so that thus he may drive us into despair, subject us to himself, and pluck us from Christ. (AE 26:10)

66. Christians are prepared to give a reason for the hope that they profess by being thoroughly grounded in God's Word. Confessing the faith is not a matter of sharing opinions about what God's Word means to me! God has given us His Word and we are to speak truthfully, rightly dividing the Law and the Gospel (see 2 Timothy 2:15).

# Appendix of Lutheran Teaching

Below you will find examples of how the first Lutherans addressed the issues of the Word. They will help you understand Lutheran spirituality. The Lutheran Confessions are accepted because they are in agreement with the Holy Scriptures. Lutheran theology holds that the Scriptures are the normative standard that norms all others (*norma normans*) and that the Lutheran Confessions are the "norm that is normed" (*norma normata)* by the Bible. Lutherans accept the authority of the Lutheran Confessions because they hold the Scriptures to be authoritative. The Book of Concord always draws us back to the Scriptures, especially to Christ, the justifier of the ungodly, who is at the heart of the Bible.

## The Word Has Divine Authority

"We believe, teach, and confess that the only rule and norm according to which all teachings, together with all teachers, should be evaluated and judged are the prophetic and apostolic Scriptures of the Old and New Testament alone" (Formula of Concord, Epitome Summary 1).

"Because we know that God does not lie. . . . God's Word cannot err" (Large Catechism IV 57).

## The Word Is the Source of Doctrine

"[This confession] . . . shows, from the Holy Scripture and God's pure Word [what is] taught in our churches" (Augsburg Confession Preface 8).

"It will not do to frame articles of faith from the works or words of the holy Fathers . . . not even an angel can do so (Galatians 1:8)" (Smalcald Articles II II 15).

"First, then, are the prophetic and apostolic Scriptures of *the Old and New Testaments* as the pure, clear fountain of Israel. They are the only true standard or norm by which all teachers and doctrines are to be judged" (Formula of Concord, Solid Declaration Summary 3, emphasis in original).

## God's Word Is a Means of Grace

"God's Word is the sanctuary above all sanctuaries. Yes, it is the only one we Christians know and have. . . . God's Word is the treasure that sanctifies everything (1 Timothy 4:5)" (Large Catechism I 91).

"So justification happens through the Word, just as Paul says in Romans 1:16, '[the Gospel] is the power of God for salvation to everyone who believes. . . . If justification happens only through the Word, and the Word is understood only by faith, it follows that faith justifies'" (Apology of the Augsburg Confession IV 67).

"We should not think of this call of God, which is made through the preaching of the Word as a juggler's act. But we should know that God reveals His will by this call. . . . It is God's will that we should receive the Word, believe it, and obey it" (Formula of Concord, Solid Declaration XI 29).

"We, too, are simply to believe . . . our Creator and Redeemer's plain, firm, clear, solemn words. . . . He can do and accomplish everything He promises" (Formula of Concord, Solid Declaration VII 47).

"In issues relating to the spoken, outward Word we must firmly hold that God grants His Spirit or grace to no one except through or with the preceding outward Word" (Smalcald Articles III VIII 3).

## God's Word Is Law and Gospel

"God's two chief works among people are these: to terrify; to justify and make alive those who have been terrified. Into these two works all Scripture has been distributed. . . . One part is the Law. . . . The other part is the Gospel" (Apology of the Augsburg Confession XII 53).

"All Scripture ought to be distributed into these two principal topics: the Law and. . . . the promises about Christ" (Apology of the Augsburg Confession IV 5).

"We unanimously believe, teach and confess . . . the distinction between the Law and the Gospel (2 Corinthians 3:6–9)" (Formula of Concord, Solid Declaration V 16–26).

# Glossary

**antinomianism.** The teaching that the Law has no place in Christian proclamation or in the life of the believer. This view was championed by John Agricola at the time of the Reformation. It was rejected by both Luther and the Lutheran Confessions as it ultimately turned the Gospel into a new law.

**cafeterianism.** An attempt to create one's own worldview by selecting, cafeteria-style, religious or moral concepts, ideas, and practices from a variety of sources. A person who attends a Christian church on Sunday while believing in reincarnation might be viewed as a "cafeterian," for example, since bodily resurrection and reincarnation are inherently incompatible.

**clarity of the Scriptures.** While not all texts in the Scriptures are equally clear, the heart and center of Scripture is Jesus Christ, who is the light of the world and makes the whole of the Bible lucid. Obscure passages are interpreted and understood in the light of those texts that are clear.

**Darwinism.** An explanation for the existence and diversity of life on earth, attributed to Charles Darwin, which includes such concepts as evolution, natural selection ("survival of the fittest"), adaptation, and other concepts.

***Deus absconditus.*** The hidden God or God as He hides Himself.

***Deus revelatus.*** The revealed God or God as He reveals Himself in Christ.

**efficacy of the Word.** The power of God's Word to effect or accomplish its divine purpose.

**enthusiasts.** A term used by Luther to refer to the radical spiritualists who believed that God came to them apart from the external instruments of Word and Sacrament.

**exegesis.** Literally "to lead or draw out" of the biblical text, to say what the text says by careful study using the original languages.

**fundamentalism.** A movement in the late nineteenth and twentieth centuries that stressed the inspiration and inerrancy of the Bible over Darwinism and other aspects of Enlightenment thought.

**Gospel reductionism.** Using the Gospel to suggest considerable latitude in faith and life not explicitly detailed in the Gospel.

**historical critical method.** An approach to the study of the Scriptures shaped by Enlightenment presuppositions regarding history and the accessibility of historical events to the interpreter. Those who practiced this method more often than not denied the divine character of the Scriptures.

**humanism.** A broad range of philosophies that emphasize human dignity and worth and recognize a common morality based on universal, rational human nature. Humanists who deny the possibility of any supernatural involvement in human affairs are sometimes called *secular* humanists.

**inerrancy.** The teaching that because the Scriptures are God's Word, inspired by the Spirit of truth, they do not lie or contain errors.

**lectionary.** A table of biblical readings (Old Testament, Epistle, and Gospel) for each Sunday and festival in the Church Year.

**modernism.** A cultural movement emerging in the late 1800s and later emphasizing the inevitability of human achievement (especially through science and technology) and a positive view of human reason, particularly in its ability to determine the truth.

**mysticism.** While mysticism itself is a broad form of spirituality with distinct nuances, it is best characterized by the movement to transcend or move above the earthly through inward experience.

*norma normans.* Literally "norming norm." This Latin term is used to describe the function of the Bible as absolutely normative in the life of the Church.

*norma normata.* Literally, "normed norm." This Latin term is used to describe the Lutheran Confessions as authoritative because they are derived from the Bible.

*postmodernism.* Refers to a cluster of themes that are somewhat interconnected in their opposition to the attempts to establish truthfulness, which characterized the period of modernity. The focus of postmodernism is characterized by pluralism and the rejection of claims to absolute truth.

*oratio, meditatio, tentatio.* Prayer, meditation, and trial. Luther said that theologians (students of God's Word) are made by prayer, meditation, and the trial of life under the cross.

**rationalism.** The Enlightenment movement that saw human reason as the ultimate criterion for reality.

**reductionism.** A *modern* concept focusing on the human ability to reduce complex ideas or things to simple or more fundamental ideas or things. *Fundamentalism* exhibits reductionism in its attempt to reduce the Christian faith to very few "key" concepts or teachings. *Gospel reductionism* makes a similar error by devaluing or outright rejecting God's Law in the life of the believer (see also *antinomianism*).

**revelation.** God's act of making His will manifest in both Law and Gospel to human beings. The instrument of God's revelation is through the prophetic and apostolic Scriptures.

*sola scriptura.* Scripture alone. Scripture is the singular fountain of Christian teaching and the final rule by which to evaluate all proclamation in the Church.

**sufficiency of Scripture.** The Scriptures are sufficient for the purpose that God gave them, namely to impart saving knowledge of Jesus Christ.

**verbal inspiration.** The teaching that God inspired the writers of the Holy Scriptures, giving them His own words to put into writing.